Give Me One Good Reason to Buy: How to Identify and Sell Your Unique Sizzle

Category: Business & Economics

Author: Bob Oros

Publisher: Bob Oros Publishing

ISBN: 978-1-387-20036-8

Copyright 2017

Description: Your customers are called on by hundreds of companies trying to sell them... Here is the key question you should always be prepared to answer... Give me one good reason why I should talk to you? Do you have one? If not, let's get to work on yours.

Key words: sales manager training, manufacturing sales training, wholesale sales training, distributor sales training, food service sales, sales coaching, sales techniques, motivating sales people, job in sales, sales course, online sales training, food sales jobs,

ISBN 978-1-387-20036-8

1. Give me one good reason to buy from you!

Having a "sizzle" is one of the most important things in both sales and marketing. If you were asked by a customer for one good reason why to buy from you, the answer would be the basis for all your sales and marketing. A complicated response will just give your potential customer another problem to sort out. Your customer does not want more to think about, they want less.

Once a really good reason is clearly defined, it should become their strongest selling point. This "one good reason" will give your selling efforts the needed "focus". It should be included in every advertisement, put on the sign, on the business card, on the brochure as well as telling everyone you come in contact with. The more you focus and promote yourself as an expert in that one area, people will assume you are good at everything else you do.

The same concept is true for sales people. If you have a really good reason why your customers should buy from you, and let them know about it on every call, your professional image will go up.

The best reason you can give is to let your customer know that your main objective is helping them become more successful and to make more money.

You are not selling simply products; you are selling additional profits, solutions to their problems, increased customer base, lower labor costs, lower product cost, etc. Many sales people use the shotgun approach trying to describe everything their company does. This is necessary at times in order to educate people as to why your company is there. It should be periodically worked into your presentations but it should never be relied on to sell products week after week.

In some instances you might want to sell the idea first and the product second. The travel business is a good example of this. They always sell the idea of travel, not necessarily the cramped six hour plane ride you have to take to get there.

Bring something new to your customers every week; it doesn't necessarily have to be a new product, only new to them. Another approach used by many successful sales people is to accent something unique about the business or your proposition. No matter how ordinary a business may seem there is always something special about it. When making your sales presentation you have to look for "points of difference" that will set you apart and attract attention at the same time.

In marketing the word "new" is used over and over again to attract attention. They are always telling about a "new ingredient" or the product is "new and improved" or it is now in a "new size".

Bringing something new to your customers week after week will show them that you are interested in their business by keeping them informed of all the things that are available.

Many buyers are totally committed to consistency and will refuse to look at a new idea even if it is in their own best interest. How can we get them to listen? One food sales manager I know has a line that never fails. "You know" he would say, "I travel a lot and eat out most of the time. Whenever I see something new on the menu I always figure they are trying to please me by giving me something new to try." Can you use this concept when putting together your sales presentations? Absolutely!

Your customers are called on by all your competitors as well as hundreds of other companies trying to sell them all kinds of products and services... Here is the key question you should always have the answer to...

Give me one good reason why I should talk to you?

How would you answer that question? What is your BIG POINT OF DIFFERENCE?

Here are some examples that you will recognize - Let me know what yours is...

M & M's – "They melt in your mouth, not in your hands."

Wonderbread – "Helps build strong bodies in 8 ways"

Crispix Cereal – "Stays crisp in milk."

Domino's Pizza – "Fresh, hot pizza delivered to your door in 30 minutes or less."

Papa John's – "Better ingredients. Better pizza. Papa John's." (before the lawsuit)

Head & Shoulders – "Healthy, beautiful, dandruff free hair."

Burger King – "Have it your way."

Oil of Olay – "Younger-looking skin."

Federal Express – "When your package absolutely, positively has to be there overnight."

Clariol – "If you use Clariol, people won't even notice that you dyed your hair."

Avis Rent a Car – "We're number two. We try harder."

Bounty – "The Quicker Picker –Upper."

Colgate – "Colgate cleans your breath while it cleans your teeth."

Geico – "Save 15 % or more on your car insurance."

State Farm – "Like a good neighbor, State Farm is there."

Enterprise –"Pick Enterprise. We'll pick you up."

Comments:

One of our long time customers said that he likes to use us because our response time is much better than any of our competitors. I have used this as my "why should I buy from you" line and it seems to be effective. Quoting a customer carries a little more credibility than the salesman saying things like "because we can solve all of your problems!" or "we can do anything you want better than anyone else!". An advertising phrase that drives me up the wall is "Simply the Best". I think it is Simply Arrogant.

Crocker Smith

Buy from me, because of me! Come across as confident, not cocky, present yourself as an accountable person, not a quick talker who makes excuses or overpromises. Let your customer know you are someone they can depend on. Don't pretend to have all the answers or that you are a magic fix to every problem they have. Don't feed them any lines. Let them know we are proud of our service offerings for a good reason. Listen to your client and do what you can to help them during a sales appointment, or do your homework to answer their questions after the appoint. If they can sense that you will work hard for for them, they will buy from you.

Marquesa Ortega

Our company has many aspects that I believe makes us better than the competitors, but the one thing that stands out above the rest is "WE DELIVER".

Lisa Lloyd

It doesn't matter if you sell products or services. You need to show and suggest ways people can do business with you. Communicate the qualities that make your business important to clients. Why should customers buy from you? They should buy because you make it easy for them to buy, you don't waste time, you make it easy for them to understand the benefits of your service, it is easy to contact you and most important you won't fail them!

Yessie Narvaez

"Why should I buy from you?" I think that is the question that goes through all potential buyers minds before you even open your mouth to speak. So as a sales person you need to be ready to answer it before they can ask it. Can't be afraid to be bold and show that you are in a different league then your competitors.

Matthew Thacker

I know the one thing we always say is if you buy from us you get "me". I think that works really well, but I do like the slogans and I think anything you can do to set yourself apart from the others and also "help" your clients in the meantime will be beneficial.

Vickie Reihl,

Customer Service should be rule number 1!! I always follow up with customers and clients to see how things are going and everything is working out. I try to always go the extra mile for each and every client. Service after the sell is very important too. Deliver on time and always do what you say your going to do....that's me!

David Bradley

"The Answer to ALL Your Foodservice Needs"

Nolen Cleaves

Our business cards are a prime example of your article. Our business cards state

"Delivering Staffing and HR Results."

A catchy slogan that might interest a Human Resource or Plant Manager. First of all our slogan indicates that we deliver and then it also states that we show results. Sometimes I tell my client that we have 3 rules of business. Customer Service, Customer service, and Customer service.

Jeffery Mole

2. How many customers do you need?

For many sales people marketing seems to be a separate division of the company with its own, unrelated agenda. However, marketing strategies can be used individually to help build your business.

The first step in marketing is to identify your target customer and determine how many customers it will take to maintain your business. Here's what I mean, using examples from different industries.

Let's say you wanted to sell residential real estate for a living. You would need to stake out an area that has a minimum of 500 houses. If you began a systematic schedule of contacting these 500 homeowners on a monthly basis, some in person, some on the phone, some by mail, there would be enough houses bought and sold each year to make a living.

Another good example is insurance. You would have to have a list of one thousand households and contact them on a regular basis. There would be enough insurance needs to earn a living. Both examples depend, of course, on your ability to out sell the competition.

Even a nursing home with one hundred beds has to have them filled with residents. If they have ten empty beds for any length of time their expenses go up and their profits go down.

A hospital is in a similar situation. The success of their marketing is measured by their "occupancy rate". The next time you call on a hospital ask what their occupancy rate is and you will be surprised at how quickly they can give you the percentage.

A manufacturer looking for national distribution needs 200 distributors.

Looking at a restaurant's business from a marketing perspective can also be measured with mathematical precision. A restaurant needing to sell a thousand meals each week to take in enough money to pay all their expenses needs a customer base of five thousand. A marketing "rule of thumb" for a restaurant is to take one week's business and multiply it times five. Restaurant customers normally rotate their eating out, so we would want to be sure that we had five thousand people "rotating" into our business at least once every five weeks.

This brings us to our basic marketing strategy as a Distributor Sales Rep (DSR). How many customers do you need and how much do you have to sell each account to make a living?

The average DSR sells a little over two million dollars each year, or $40,000 each week. The average order size in the industry is $500. That means to be "average" you would have to sell 80 accounts $500 every week. NOT A GOOD PLAN!

What if we double the order size to $1,000? That brings the number of accounts down to 40. Forty accounts purchasing $1,000 each week sounds better, however, we are still only "average".

Let's give it one more twist. Let's weed out the low margin price shoppers and carefully select 40 accounts that could buy at least $2,000 per week from you. Now you are investing your time and effort with accounts that will give you sales exceeding four million dollars per year.

It look's good on paper, as all marketing plans do. However, it is still up to you to make it happen the old fashioned way, by selling.

Comments:

My goal is to determine the dollar amount from your game plan I need monthly to maximize profits. If you follow some type of "plan" daily you remain in contact with current customers and stay on top of new prospects. Going after the most profitable prospects is a good idea. Sometimes the larger the order the less the profit becomes. Typically you give some type of "discount" to become a company's only vendor. Customers that only use minimal services I provide may be more a profitable account. You have to weigh your options and follow through with achieving your goal, and keep selling. Everyone can always use more customers!

Brooke Knight

I think you do need to know the base number of accounts you need to sell every month to maintain your business, however, you constantly need backups in case you loose a client or their business slows down. But, I don't think that your base number should be your "goal", your goals should be set higher than what you need to maintain your business so you continue to grow.

Vickie Reihl

I see the process of building of clientele as a road map. You know your ultimate goal. You figure out the best way to get there. Your plan needs to include contingencies and have enough space that you can deal with emergencies or problems and still move forward. And sometimes, the plan changes so it might need some adjustment. As long as the goal remains the same and as long as you keep taking steps forward to achieve that goal, your plan will help you get there. The key is to ask yourself where you want be in the future and how you plan to get where you want to be.

Yessenia Narvaez

Our company has implemented a strategy to see how many companies we need in our customer base to keep the wheel turning. Each branch needs to have approximately 150 pre-qualified companies in the 90 day planner to plan your calls for the week. The larger target accounts will be visited at least once a week with the smaller classification accounts being contacted bi-weekly or monthly. This is a great way to plan your week and to make sure you follow up with each client in a timely manner.

Gregg Nixon

I think you do need to know the base number of accounts you need to sell every month to maintain your business, however, you constantly need backups in case you loose a client or their business slows down. But, I don't think that your base number should be your "goal", your goals should be set higher than what you need to maintain your business so you continue to grow.

Vickie Reihl

I think that's always been the big debate in sales. How many clients do we need? In most industries it can be broken down into a nice neat dollar amount. Hopefully this will make your goal. In other industries it isn't so clean. You may have a client that spends $500 a week or another client that does $3,000 a week. I think it is a matter of acquiring the correct type of client. We also have to remember that it isn't always the big client that spends the $3000 that will be with you for the long haul, it might be the small client of $500 that stays with you year after year. I don't think there is a magical number to how many clients we need, we need a lot of clients as salespeople, the more we have the better we do. After all at some point in time a customer might not "order" for a while.

Brandon Sanchez

I need to have approximately 150 full-time working employees at any given time to meet my projected sales budget. If I have more great. If I have less, not so great.

That is why I am constantly selling. In my line of work, the selling never stops. I must sell daily, weekly, monthly, and yearly. I must sell during business hours as well as after business hours. My sales hat never comes off. I wear it at church or the local grocery store. When I am talking to anyone, I want them to be thinking "she knows her stuff" I want them to see that I always have time for them and that I am the same out of work as I am at work. I look at every person as a potential customer. You never know who may be where tomorrow in today's highly fluctuating job market. But I love what I do, and I know where I will be.

Kathie Luttrell

3. What questions do you ask to design your presentation?

Before making a presentation ask yourself the following questions:

1. Do you have a price advantage or a price problem?

If you do not have an advantageous price, don't say a thing about price. Make sure that your benefits are strong enough to get people interested so that when you follow up directly they will be sufficiently interested to pay a higher price.

2. Who is the person who will buy your product or service?

There's no substitute for actually talking with prospects and customers to see what motivates them to buy your products or those of your competitors. Every situation is different, and you can make the most of your selling and marketing efforts if you make your presentation to the person that can be most influential in the sale.

3. What are the economic benefits of using your product?

If you can say that your product or service will save the customer money, time, or effort, you have a great competitive advantage. If you can document this with figures you'll have a very persuasive story to tell. Don't be afraid to go into the details. If your customer is even the

21

least bit cost conscious, they will listen to every word of your presentation.

4. What is the product made of or what does the service consist of?

Carefully study the product or service you are going to sell. If it is a product, get all the details on how it is made, what it is made of, etc. If it is a service, describe exactly what the service consists of. Write out the description as if you were explaining it to a young child who knew absolutely nothing about it.

5. What does the product or service do best?

All products have several features and benefits that will appeal to prospects. Before you say a word, determine which of the benefits will be most important to the largest segment of your market. Keep in mind that a feature is a fact about the product or service and a benefit is what the feature will do for the customer. People buy benefits, not features.

6. How important are your competitive differences?

Your product or service may be better than that of a competitor on a point that doesn't make any real difference to the person who must make the choice. Don't be fooled into using this advantage as a benefit. Even if you do have a great competitive advantage over other products, never knock the competitors. But do make sure that your reader knows the difference and appreciates what it will mean if your product is bought.

Comments:

This all boils down to "know what your customer is looking for". I had one customer who hardly looked at price. He was only interested in the finance rate and monthly payments. Another had enough cash to buy our whole company so finance meant little to him. Still another had been burned by a competitor's service department so he wanted a company that would stand behind him and support the product.

I have gotten many sales by knowing what to stress in the negotiations and I have also lost sales when my competitor knew more than me.

Crocker Smith

The questions that I ask myself before making a presentation are "Who do I have to talk to?"- The decision maker. Sometimes you can talk all day to the wrong person and only waste both of your time. "How can my service benefit this particular client?" Then I can customize my presentation to client by client basis. "What are any competitive differences or concerns?" Be able to address this topic without talking bad about the competition. "What about my price versus competitions price?" I need to be able to justify my service, my quality. I use this as my outline for my presentation.

Brooke Knight

Pretend you were pitching it to yourself. What or how you would like someone to make a sales pitch to you and what would influence you to buy from them. Then take that and use it on your next client.

David Bradley

This all goes back to talking and then listening to your client. They know best what they want and you and I know best as to what we are selling. We have to constantly compete against similar companies that sale the same product/service. This is when we acknowledge the great industry we are in and how many other companies are good at what they do. We then need to let the client know why we can do it a little better without slamming the others.

We have to listen and we have to believe in the service we are selling, if we don't buy it why would anyone else?

Brandon Sanchez

The primary point is preparation. Sales people will go to a potential buyer to make a presentation and some with little to no knowledge of what they're selling or why they're selling it. Know the customer's wants and needs and try and direct the benefits of your product to their needs. Know what you're selling. In order to sale productively you must know the ends and outs of the product and believe in what you're selling.

Matthew Thacker

Before any type of a presentation I give close people permission for an honest opinion or suggestions that will help me improve my presentation. I believe that we do not have to act on every suggestion but we do need to carefully try to consider every suggestion out there that would help us prepare the right presentation for the right audience. I don't consider myself the best presenter, but at least I have a road map and I am working on making progress toward my goal.

Yessie Narvaez

I always want to know the companies expectations. How much personal contact do you want me to have with the employee's? Do you mind frequent on-site visits? (I have actually had the employee of client ask me questions because they saw me so much they thought I worked there.) I let them know that if I am going to serve them, I want to do it right. Many times I have had a potential client mention a problem with a competitor as a reason for not doing business with me. And I agree with your "don't knock the competition" philosophy. I think it is low and unprofessional. I simply state that I am not associated with that company and if given the chance I can prove the difference. The presentation should be your knock their socks off with what you can offer extravaganza. I especially love it when at the end of a presentation a client says something like I better watch out or all of my staff may want to work for you. No matter what you ask a client you won't get every client on the first or even second try, but don't give up and when you get your chance show them what they have been missing.

Kathie Luttrell

I guess it goes without saying that you should know as much as you possibly can about a product or service that you are selling, but one should also give some thought to the situation, or people in which this product or service will be used or used by.....really try and see what makes them tick, or what is important to them. One needs to ask questions before hand to know the answers before you go in.

Jonathan Kendig

4. How do you set your price?

You may have little choice. If your market facts tell you that all your competitors are selling the same item at one dollar, and if one dollar is the absolute least you can charge and still survive, then the decision makes itself. This, however, is rare; you usually have some flexibility.

Your price (less costs) sets your gross profit--at least on that one sale. Very few businesses, of course, can survive on just one sale. So your gross profit, in actuality, is based on your price, multiplied by your number of units of sale, minus your costs.

Some customers buy on price alone, or with price as a key factor. A very few ignore price completely. Most seek the greatest value, real or imagined, per dollar. This factor is usually known as "perceived value." The "ceiling" and the "floor" are terms that describe the highest and lowest possible price decisions you can make. Your ceiling might be what your competition is offering; your floor might be the lowest price you can charge and still turn a profit.

Sometimes, you may wish, briefly, to sell near or below your cost, in order to get customers to try your product or service. Eventually, of course, you must sell above your cost in order to build gross profit--that is, the dollars that allow you to keep your business in operation.

If you are more efficient than your competitor, you might sell below their price and still generate enough income to pay all your other costs and still end up with a net (or bottom line) profit. If you do sell below your competitor's price, you will probably aim to sell enough extra units to make up for the lost income from lower price. Your gross will very likely be lower than the competitor's on each individual sale. By the same token, higher real or perceived value can let you sell above your competition's price. This can cut your number of units sold just as a lower price raised them. However, if you can compensate for the reduction by the extra dollars you will see with a higher price, income goes up.

Pricing should be a window, not a barrier. For instance, volume discounts to key larger customers usually increase your efficiency and profitability, and thus represent a reasonable basis for a price reduction.

Clearly, your decision can be a little tricky. Your price should probably be somewhere between your cost and your competitor's price. If you decide to charge more than a competitor, you need to have reasons that justify the higher price and/or a superior product or service.

Comments:

In the final analysis, the company that can control costs will always control the market.

Jim Ruth

"Different strokes for different folks" is an old saying that goes pretty well when it comes to pricing your customers. It all depends on how much competition you have in the various accounts and what their pricing structure is. In some accounts it may be easy to get your full book price and in others you may have to discount prices in order to stay competitive. The most important thing is the overall picture and to keep in mind that without profits there is no commissions.

Phil Hackett

A company I sold for competed against the industry leader for many years and customers would pay a large premium just for the name on the product. Over the years we were able to increase our good reputation while offering a much better value for the dollar. We did not make much profit but our market share steadily rose and the competitor was forced to start lowering prices. Eventually the prices became almost the same but our market share continued to increase. We slowly began increasing our gross profit and the trend continued. Even though they continued to be the market leader, we closed the gap and made more money.

Crocker Smith

Setting your price on your product is based on the quality and performance that your product provides. If your price is higher that the competition, you have to be able to justify why. You have let the buyer see what and how much they are getting for there money and how much better it is that the other guys. Remember, you get what you pay for!!

David Bradley

Either way you will have to work hard to make sales. If you charge more for a product you will have to work hard to show the clients the features and benefits of your product over competitors. If you charge less then you have to make more sales calls to make the up the difference in sales numbers.

Brian Spraggins

Prices should not be set in stone. I believe that making sales would be very difficult if there was absolutely no negotiating. I work in staffing so it is a little bit hard to be flexible on my price. The biggest area we can flex is when it comes to the quantity of business they project to do with us. If they will be doing consent business with us then we can charge them at a lower percentage whereas someone that wanted to do business with us for 2 weeks we would need to charge more. Price should be flexible but you shouldn't break yourself to get a sale.

Matthew Thacker

You pretty much educate your customers and the price should fit in. I totally agree that the best and safest way to set your prices is by comparing your prices with your competitors and to make sure that is not lower than your cost. By doing that, you will make sure that you are not under pricing your product or services.

Yessenia Narvaez

When considering a reduced price I feel it is important to calculate how it will affect your profit. If the volume makes up the difference then that would be one thing. On the other hand to get your foot in the door I would never reduce below a competitor because it runs the risk of being stuck in that fee range long term or the word on how cheap you are will be generated through out referrals which will expect the same reduction.

Carla McCrea

Well, if we're talking about a competitive situation where the customer is giving you an opportunity to get the business based on price then the trick is to try to determine where that point is…you don't want to leave money "on the table," so to speak. Often the customer will tell you what they are paying, and in such cases I try to come up with a price that satisfies the "perceived value" for the customer, and allows me to make a profit.

Jonathan Kendig

While selling low at first then hoping that eventually you can sell for higher is a great thought in theory. But in all actuality it seems that people want the discounts after buying initially. We can get a contract at a high rate and then I have seen it over and over, after a few months the competition comes in and tries to underbid us, and then our phone rings well so and so can do it for this can you match or we will switch to ABC Company. That is so frustrating.

Morgan Frazier

5. What does your price tell your customer?

With effective, intelligent pricing, you can out-maneuver, out-market, and out-sell your competitor and get a bigger share of the market.

1. More products fail because of a price that is too low, than because of a price that is too high.

2. It is easier to cut prices than raise them.

3. "Prestige" pricing can often build your perceived value.

4. One particularly effective strategy is to start out with a relatively high "prestige" price, then cut the price later. The result is a high perceived level of quality, plus a "value" look.

5. A low (or "defensive") price can discourage new competitors.

6. Price testing with a sample group of customers is an excellent way to get important information. Check for positive or negative reactions at various price levels.

7. Price in such a way that you build up your bottom line.

8. Do not get involved in price conspiracy or price fixing agreements.

9. Your pricing strategy should attract customers and confuse competitors.

Price is a vitally important element in your market strategy. You can usually change it quickly, unlike your product or its packaging.

Comments:

I think when looking at pricing, we need to keep in mind what it means to us when we are out personally shopping for products. Sometimes low pricing makes us think that it is poor quality; higher prices sometimes represent higher quality. People will often pay more for well known, quality brand names, or specialty items and not question it because they are aware of its value. Always being at the lowest point is not necessarily the place to be. Like you said sometimes it's better to start higher and negotiate down, rather than being at the bottom right off the bat.

Kristen Storer

I think the key here is "perceived value" by the customer. If they believe that they are getting more for their dollar they will pay a higher price. But if you don't meet their expectations based on what they paid it will be a one time sale.

What really confuses the issue is when a new competitor comes in and is prepared to lose money by buying the business. Some customers find that irresistible but, in the long run, they usually come back to the overall best value.

Crocker Smith

These are some great strategies to use in any market of sales. Usually price is the main issue when it comes to making or closing the deal. You have to use these strategies carefully though! This can come back to haunt you later. To low of a price can make a potential client curious or weary of making the purchase. Be careful when messing around with price. Find out what is competitive in your market and go from there!

David Bradley

I believe that price is a good selling point to get your clients attention. If you price your product to low it lessens the value, and if your price is to high it will turn them off. The trick I think is to price your product at such a point that the client will say to them selves that it is a bit high but they must have a good product to be so confident to charge at this price point.

Brian Spraggins

Its true, if we go too low what does that tell our client. They will think one of two things; wow that's a real deal or wow what's wrong with your service you can offer it so cheap. We need to be willing to start out at a price that we fill is competitive in our market and stand by it letting our service and dedication prove it to the client. We also have to remember that it is very difficult to have a customer be ok with us constantly increasing prices, and that's what will happen if we start too low. Costs go up every year, we need to give us a little padding to grow as well.

Brandon Sanchez

You're price will say a lot about you. In anything that I buy personally, I am very leery about buying something that's much cheaper than competitors. To me, it raises the question, "what's wrong with it?" On the other hand you can't out price yourself right from the start. People will pay more for better service, but if it's that much more they'll just stick with what they have. If you know that your price is higher going into a presentation, sale them on the benefits before anyone can even mention price.

Matthew Thacker

Some customers might feel prices are unfair and it is very hard to correct those perceptions. Even when we use certain techniques to remind or educate customers about our company's costs or benefits, we can only change a small percentage of their opinions. Our price could tell a lot of things to customers, our job is to investigate their opinion and reactions to the price. For example, high prices originated from high quality seem to be fair to some customers, but high prices based for other reasons are usually less fair to other customers, and some customers are just willing to pay more than others. The reasons they base their buying decisions is what help us see what they think of our price. If we know what they think, then we can compete in the market.

Yessie Narvaez

Our lives revolve around price and negotiating prices, from buying a new car, to selecting a high speed internet plan. We are surrounded by choices of prices. We must know our client before quoting prices. Boils back down to research. We don't want to seem to high, or too low.

Kimberly Burgess

When presenting a high price always have the ability to justify, then if necessary you are able to lower. When quoting the high or standard price it shows your confidence in your service / product. When starting with a lower price, buyers will question the quality of the service or product. It will raise doubts in their mind as to the actual benefits of purchasing or what is wrong with this picture. Plus once you start lower you can't go anywhere but down.

Carla McCrea

It is difficult to deal with low cost buyers, the ones who will buy the cheapest, because it's cheap with no consideration on any other factor. If they do eventually buy your product they are so cheap they will nickel and dime you to death. Also I don't' want you to want my product because it's cheap, I want you to want my product because it's the best, and I am the best.

Morgan Frazier

6. What is the one skill all successful sales people use?

An airplane flying from Chicago to NY is off course as much as 97% of the time, however the pilot keeps adjusting and making corrections.

The first step for a sales person to stay on course is to make a list of the things you have to do tomorrow and number them in the order of importance.

You have to continually monitor your progress to make sure you are heading in the right direction, or in case you have to change and adjust your plan.

Selling is unlike many other professions in that you have to keep yourself motivated and organized on a daily basis. Many other types of work are built on the routine of doing something over and over again, however, selling requires a review of your battle plan every day or, at times, every hour.

You have your over all objectives as well as the accounts you must see on any given week, but as you begin each day you have new situations and opportunities that did not exist yesterday.

The most important thing you can do at the end of each day is make a list of the things you have to do tomorrow and number them in the order of importance. It is important to do it at the end of each day. If you wait until morning you may forget an important item. Also by doing it at the end of the day your subconscious mind will have a chance to work on your list during the night and help you solve your problems while you sleep.

Things will come up to change our program, however, a numbered list will give you a track to run on and will keep you working on the most important things first.

To stay on course spend one hour each day or four hours each week carefully planning each sales call you are going to make.

Planning is one of the most important activities of a sales person. The shorter the time we have to spend with each customer, the more important it is that we carefully go over each step of our sales plan.

Winston Churchill was once asked how long it would take him to prepare for a 10 minute speech. He said he would like at least a month's notice. When asked how far in advance for a one hour speech he said at least a week, and when asked how long he needed to prepare for a four hour talk he said he could start now.

He made an excellent point for planning sales presentations. To make an effective 10 minute presentation takes careful planning and organizing. If you were going to spend four hours with a customer it would not be necessary to spend a lot of preparation time because everything you want to discuss will come out in the course of the four hours.

A professional sales person will spend at least one hour in planning time for each day of selling. It takes that much time to write letters, make appointments, prepare presentations and carefully think about the details of each call we are going to make.

Staying on course takes practice. Just as the airline pilot has to go through months and months of training, so do sales people.

Many times a sales person does not have the advantage of being a "co-pilot" with the opportunity to study under an experienced "pilot". This is one of the reasons selling has such a high failure rate. It is a lonely, difficult job. However, that is why the rewards are so great.

Comments:

I firmly believe in the "having no plan is a plan to fail' montra. It is vitally important to know with whom you need to speak, what their "hot" buttons are, and knowing what they look to achieve. There is no way to know these things without planning. You cannot make an effective presentation without the proper plan. And remember......your first 30 seconds IS and probably the MOST important presentation. You cannot make a sale in the first 30 seconds of meeting someone, but you can certainly lose one.

Bill Hatfield

Getting an early start to my day I find is the best thing I can do because like you said as a sales person, you can run off track very easily. Getting a good start to the day, knocking off tasks on my "to do list" quickly in the morning, helps leave time later in the day for unexpected things as they come up... and they do come up. I try to make a list, keep notes and use my day planner as much as possible to ensure I don't forget to do something on the day I need to do it. As unexpected things come up throughout the day, it is very easy to forget to do something if it is not written down somewhere on the day it needs to be taken care of.

I think being organized is something I can be continually working on and I find new ways of organizing myself all the time. Last week I started using the voice memo on my phone to help make a list of things I need to do while I am driving. I find a lot of times when I am on the road I do nothing but think of all of the things I have to do that are not written down and I worry I may forget something. This helps me remember by repeating these tasks out loud to myself and it is recorded so I can refer back to it later in the day if needed.

Kristen Storer

Sometimes I am only allowed 30 seconds to state my purpose in front of a potential customer. I have to plan and tailor my words to immediately appeal to that customer and make me stand out from the competition.

Having your sales calls mapped out when you start is a great stress reliever and also saves gas.

Crocker Smith

I don't think you can do too much planning and being flexible with your plan when you are in sales. But, making your list of the most important things will definitely help you stay on track and get more accomplished. I appreciate all the good information you are giving me.

Vickie Reihl

Careful planning is needed to make almost every sales call a success. Plan each day in advance and schedule yourself enough time to get to all your appointments and have enough time to spend with each client. Planning your day the day before can be a big help. By waiting till the morning before, there is a good possibility that you are going to forget something that you need to do or follow up on from the day before.

David Bradley

I completely agree with this. I am constantly making notes and lists all day every day. It might be in a notebook, folder or a board. When we as sales people get busy we need to attempt in every way possible to keep organized. I have found out, especially lately, that I need to make lists in order to accomplish everything. This hasn't always been the case. But at times we get very busy and it's necessary to stay organized in order for everything to get accomplished. Post It Notes and dry erase boards are lifesavers.

Brandon Sanchez

Planning is the one skill that all successful sales people must possess. I haven't been in sales long, but I don't believe that it's possible to be successful in this business if you spend everyday just "winging it." I have learned that utilizing every minute of the day is so important. Most the time, there aren't enough hours in the day, so wasting any time can really hurt. In order to utilize all of your time you must have a plan.

Matthew Thacker

Planning ahead of time is like a roadmap. You just need to follow it or change it if necessary to get you where you want to go. Planning your obligations take the frustration out of the day. It assures you that the necessary things get done and get done on time. Learn what you want to accomplish. Your can have whatever you want, but you must enough to do the things that have to be done to get it. The main thing is to plan your work then work your plan!

Yessie Narvaez

Having a numbered list of activities that I must complete each day gives me structure and keeps me on track. In the recruiting world there are so many things that can occur at any given time through out the day that can distract you. As

I complete the tasks listed I also get the feeling of accomplishment. The days when I mark only a few I don't have the same feeling. It will add stress until I get back on track.

Carla McCrea

This is where the 90 day planner comes into play. Just making sure if you call a client and told them you will follow up in a week, then do it!! Every salesperson needs to understand they have to be their own motivator. Sometimes sales people have those days where you just don't feel like making those sales calls. You are the only person that is going to kick your butt to do something about it. Yes the rewards can be endless depending on how hard you work.

Danah Parmley

Planning and organization are the key to success, in many situations. Sometime planning can be very detailed and difficult sometimes it will just take a second get you thoughts together and resume whatever the task is. I do think that planning for a 10 minute presentation is much harder than an hour long presentation. Because you have to fit and hours worth of talking and dealing into 10 minutes.

Morgan Frazier

7. How do you set yourself apart from your competition?

The first step in setting yourself apart is to make a commitment to really be on top of your business. A daily to-do system, writing everything down in one place, carrying out your promises, returning all customer calls within two to three hours, checking voice mail every two or three hours and updating your message, sending follow up notes and letters, notifying customers of bad news, delays and coming up with alternatives. All these things are under your direct control.

One of the best ways to gain credibility with a prospect is to promise to do something-and to do it. Poor self-management is the cause of poor results. Salespeople who don't succeed usually don't have a system. They don't write things down. If they have a list, they don't use it. Not taking initiative also contributes to problems. The key is to identify what you can control and act on it.

Today the business of selling is more complex, and involves continuous service. More can go wrong. It is fairly unusual to get a fast decision when calling on a new prospect. Although some sales can be split-second, with the customer saying yes or no on the spot, most new account sales don't happen that way. Typically, you are one of several competitors. Normally you are trying to take business away from a competitor. And throughout this kind of selling process attention to detail plays a big role.

Taking care of the details during the process of trying to open a new account can make or break the possibility of future business. Telephone calls, letters, or personal visits can put you ahead of less attentive competitors. Many salespeople are poor at this type of work. So being precise in your attention to details can put you in a very favorable position.

Attention to detail plays an important roll, once the sale is in place, to help insure nothing goes wrong. After the sale make sure it's not your last order with this customer. Consider yourself successful if you learn in time that things are not going well. Meeting and exceeding customer expectations will allow you to move up to partner. How well you deliver on your sales promise will build your reputation with your customer and his or her colleagues. It will help you get "add-on" business. Always develop a "deliver more than you promise" attitude. This strategy is called UPOD. Under promise, over deliver.

If you make it a point to be meticulous about the details, you will be able to differentiate yourself from your competitors. You can count on some of your competitors letting small things slip by them.

As we discussed in Report 17, Having a sense of urgency, this can also be used as a way to set yourself apart from your competitors.

Let's review and ask that question again to signify the importance of doing thing right now!

Do you call your customers when there is a potential problem? When you hear a piece of news that could possibly affect one of your customer's business do you make it a special point to let them know, or do you assume they will get the information themselves?

When one of your customers has a problem and calls you for help, do you drop everything and do "what ever it takes" to help with the solution, or do you hesitate and hope that by the time you return the call the problem will go away?

If your answer is yes to these questions, you are in the top ten percent!

Comments:

In the heat of a sales call you want the sale so bad you can find yourself moving away from UPOD and moving towards OPUD Over Promise Under Deliver. Keep in mind

Murphy's Law will be in the room sooner than later. You work hard to get the sale, now you've got to do the day to day work to keep it! One order does not make a life long client!

David Vize

If you do the right thing.....and we all know what the "right thing" is....we will usually come out ahead. Sometimes it is easy to rationalize not doing the "right thing" when it's not convenient to do so. If there is a twinge of guilt with your response, then you know you haven't done the "right thing."

Jonathan Kendig

It's important for any salesperson to do what the say they are going to do! Deliver on time and check in to see how everything is going. You have to keep track of who you have spoken to and what was said to that person. Follow up after the sale is very important to. Always let the client know what you can and cant do. If you cant make something happen or deliver on time, then you need to let the client know instead of keeping them guessing. Return calls promptly and do whatever it takes to make the client happy and keep them happy.

David Bradley

I definitely do everything in my power to follow through on what I say. If I have a client or prospective client that asks me to contact them in a week, I have it scheduled to call them back in a week. They have already requested I contact them again and now the ball is in my court and all I have to do is what they need me to, and that's follow through on my promise. I do drop everything to help my clients. I recently had a couple different clients that were in need of some replacement employees. I stopped what I was doing in order to fill those positions. By me doing this we are able to secure future business with those clients because they know we deliver. That's how we set ourselves apart.

Brandon Sanchez

You have to name each 'twin' differently to give it a very distinct identity. When you do that, your client recognizes the difference and chooses that 'twin' for its own individual personality and character. If you feel the difference so does your client and to ignore this basic human instinct is to do so at your own.

Yessie Narvaez

I once heard a sales person say, "Customer service means nothing. Customer satisfaction is where sales come from." Plan, execute, and follow up are the keys to setting yourself apart from your competitors. Setting yourself apart means exceeding where your competitors will fall short.

Matthew Thacker

As we frequently say here, do it right the first time. And as I always say to my children, if you take a short cut in life, your life will be cut short. We should say what we mean, and mean what we say. Doing it right from the beginning sets us apart from our competition.

Kimberly Burgess

Excellent customer services is the key to setting me and our company above the competitor. I have gained and kept more business by paying attention to details and being attentive to the needs, and more importantly the wants of my clients. I want each of my clients feel like they are the most important to me. I have said many times that a client lost is much harder to regain than trying to get a new client.

Lisa Lloyd

Putting the customers' needs first is one of the most important things a sales person can do. Our company has the motto, "Do whatever it takes" and it makes perfect sense. If you go out of your way to help /assist your customer in as many areas as possible they will become as loyal to you as you are to them. Following up and staying on top of things where they are considered will result in you reaping the rewards.

Carla McCrea

I believe follow-ups are key ways that set me apart from my competitors. Everyday after sales calls I follow up with either a phone call, email, or a letter. This keeps me fresh on their mind and it also shows them I am already committed.

Heath Blanchard

Responding quickly to problems or being proactive and interested in our customer's success is crucial to out long term success. In our office we do "whatever it takes" to give them what they want and need. All the while satisfying the applicant's needs and wants as well, it's pretty awesome when it all goes hand in hand.

Morgan Frazier

This is one area I believe I am very strong in. As one of your follow ups mentioned. One of my personal pet peeves is not answering or getting back to a customer. As a customer it would drive me crazy waiting to get a response. I have realized sometimes I am to quick to respond, I know that sounds strange but it happens quite often. Just today I had a customer call me to let me know he didn't get an item but he was billed for it. I called our driver and he had already returned with the item.

I try to put myself in the place of the customer and try and to figure out what I would expect and go from there.

Dominick Yarnal

Customer service, customer service, and more customer service. You have to remain flexible with yourself and your service. My #1 pet peeve in business is when you leave someone a message and they do not call you back. I can handle anything but this. Always follow through with your promises, voicemails, emails, and etc. Be as honest with the client as possible.. This directly relates to making promises. Do not tell a customer you can do something before checking to see if it is allowable by the corp office. Tell a customer that you are not sure about that and you will get back to him in a timely manner.   The worst thing you can do is not check on it and not call him back. Learn to listen and realize that every customer is as important as the next. I sometimes tell myself that the client is my employer. Without them I would not have food on the table, clothes on my back, and a descent home for my family.

Jeffrey Mole

About the author Bob Oros

Regardless of whether you are reading one of his books or attending one of his programs, the most frequent comment is: "This guy has been there, he is one of us, I am going to use these strategies."

With over 2,000 speaking engagements in all 50 states and several international locations for manufacturers, distributors and associations, you can be sure you will get the results and information you are looking for. Prior to starting his speaking career, Bob served six years in the US Navy as a Communications Specialist and then worked his way from a street sales person to the position of National Sales Manager for a Fortune 200 company.

Bob has received awards for speaking, writing and marketing too numerous to mention.

Additional Topics by Bob Oros

Why Sales People Fail

The Key to Selling Anybody

The Power of Expectations

Add Value to Every Product

How to Justify Your Price

Lost in 60 Seconds

One Good Reason to Buy

Control a Buyer's Attitude

How to Create Demand

Smoke Screen Objections

Take the Risk Out of Sales

How Small Companies Get Big